The Victims of Lifelong Slavery

The Weak Vessels

By

Bernard Benson Sarfo

Also by Bernard Benson Sarfo

The Fact Among Facts (1st)
The Fact Among Facts

Standalone
The Youth Murderer
Be Original Not a Copy
The Christians Science or Scholarship
Precious than Paradise
Habit Makes Future
A shelter from storm and rain
The Science of Life
The Strongest Lion Knockback
The Perfect and Inspiring City
Above Hope, Faith and Love
The Hero's Brave Decisions
The Weakest Among Plants
The Hero's Brave Decisions
Doing Above The Ability
The Wisdom Beyond Power And Greatness
Heavier Than the Heavens
The Academics Brains and Recreation Logics
The Strange Voice

Dedication

I dedicate this book to everyone in the world today and wish them courage!

'When wisdom entered into your heart, and knowledge is pleasant unto your soul, discretion shall preserve you, understanding shall keep you' (Proverbs 2:10, 11).

Introduction

The journey of Israelites in the wilderness for forty years; is the journey for every Christian. Let every Christian take note of that, without hardship, there will be no good fruit expecting from the tree will be attained.

The presence of sin has lost the right choice of a man by which he can be redeemed. We need to experience proper condition of life to make us alive again through hardships.

Let us learn something from the Israelites through their wilderness life and then to understand our Christian life whiles we are journey towards Heaven. We are all the victims of lifelong slavery because of the sin of our first parents.

The idea of God for this world at the beginning has changed due to the sin committed by man. Death has taken place and the man has become useless due to that condition.

The earth was curse through the sin of man. This issue needs a change by circumstances that will fight against the sin from overcoming. So, God allow hardship to make a way for proper condition to change the situation that sin has made it occur.

In order for a man to live better and comfortable life, there must a circumstance to pave a way for slight enjoyment. Else, the whole life of a man will experience bitterness throughout his life last.

Therefore, it became necessary for a man to suffer for want and needs in his life sometimes to make things right. This is the way by which God can redeem a man for the purpose by which He created man to be.

The purpose of life is now subjected to hardships or circumstances for a man to make right choice with carefulness. Due to the will, and the freedom of a choice that man have. For us to be necessary and needful for God's work, circumstances must be permitted by Him to refine a man.

This is the solution by which God allow for us to seek Him and to make our friendship regain it stands. Else, the man will not have or think that he needs God help through his life due to sin condition he has encountered. He works in us to will and to do for His good pleasure.

So, God took Abraham and his children to teach the entire world or people of the world the purpose of life and His intention towards them. He led Israel to be a slave in Egypt and then again brought them to His choice of land.

Oh how can a baby live alone without his or her mother guidance? Who have been able to live without mother or father before?

Who has not been child before? Can a man produce children without a woman? Can one man build a whole city without other hands?

It is impossible to live without God or survive without air? Elisha considered God in his life and thought he cannot live without Him. He asked for the Spirit of God in his life and then determined to live with God.

We need this kind of the spirit that Elisha had to live. He called out God of Elijah to be his help in his journey. God answered him at the right time. He is ever ready to help us if we will call Him.

We are not alone, He is always with us to support and sustain. Only if we will recognize him, He shall assist and then give all the needs.

Elisha proclaimed; where is the Lord God of Elijah? And God answered him. Who knows the purpose of God in his or her life?

Your life has been planned by God for greater responsibilities and it needs discipline to grow in the direction He (God) want it. You need to go through fire for purification and forcefulness of God's work.

Your shadows have a purpose and the reasons of those circumstances. Do not doubt but be hopeful. You are great man, and your life needs experience for your responsibilities.

Do not challenge or annoy that you can do by your own strength. I have seen that, no one can survive without air, so it is that; without God no one can live. Many think that, it is by their power that they exist.

Your life is not yours that you can do for your own best. It is not in your hands to control air to move in the direction you want it. You are nothing and you cannot be anything without God.

It is not by power or strength to do; but by His Spirit. If I challenge, I will fail without His aid. Without Christ you can do nothing. You cannot; dare, to do without God.

If you challenge, you will fail. Our only hope and life is Christ. Without Him no one will be accepted by God. It is not by our strength but by His grace that we live and have our being.

As the world came by the power and the word of God; so we can survive and have our being through His word. Without Him we cannot survive. Do not challenge that it is by your own strength.

It is not but by His grace. You shall be fruitless without His aid and you will be as nothing without His grace. You are not alone; your creator is still holding you and cares for you. He will not forget you or forsake you.

He knows the thought He has for you. It is a thought of peace but not of evil to give hope and future with abundance. You cannot; dare, walk alone. You shall fail by your own strength but you will win by His strength and power.

He has prepared everything necessary for your life and wishes you well. What you need is to trust Him and depend on Him.

He will not leave you nor forsake you. It is not your duty to care for yourself, but it is your duty only to trust and obey Him. You shall not flop.

In all, we are not alone but someone is always near to us. As Christians, we should not worry at all. We have God who cares and He is always near to help and rescue us from all dangers. We are not alone, God is always with us.

It is interesting to note that, those who are not of God are loved by God. Whether they will choose Him or not; we are not alone wherever we are, God is always with us. In our lives, sometimes it seems we are left alone to suffer and struggle for ourselves.

We sometimes feel misery and mischief. We always lost hope when things went wrong. But there is one who sees our troubles and sufferings. He will not leave us or forsake us. He cares and always wants to help and delivered.

We need to have hope and take heart. God knows our problems and miseries and He is always near to support us from our troubles. Do not think that God has left you to struggle by your effort, It is not so.

He is near to support and to provide. He knows your sufferings and he is willing to assist and rescue. Do not be afraid, God is with you until the end of the world.

So, take heart and be at peace. It is not all lost but it shall be well. Have faith in God and keep on going. Do not stop but move forward; there is hope at the end. Worrying is blind and it cannot see the future. Those who entertain it suffer for no improvement.

It is not good to be faithless but it is good to be hopeful and be at peace. You need to trust God and then have faith in Him. He knows your troubles and grief. Do not be afraid, He is always near to help. Be at peace!

Contents

12. **It is now dark in my life**
13. **Show me the way**
14. **Do not leave me, Please!**
15. **Are you troubled?**
16. **What are you looking for?**
17. **Are you wondering?**
18. **Does God care?**
19. **Why all these troubles?**
20. **It shall be well**
21. **He is waiting to hear you**
22. **Do not be afraid**

1. Our Situation today

The world has lessons for us as human beings due to the presence of sin. It is difficult to understand how sin came yet it is through our first parent disobedient.

This condition has made the life much bitter and hard to live. We are all crying due to our situation today. The world has changed through the existence of sin and the sin originator.

The idea of God for this world at the beginning has changed due to the sin committed by man. Death has taken place and the man has become useless due to that condition.

The earth was curse through the sin of man. This issue needs a change by circumstances that will fight against the sin from overcoming. So, God allow hardship to make a way for proper condition to change the situation that sin has made it occur.

In order for a man to live better and comfortable life, there must a circumstance to pave a way for slight enjoyment. Else, the whole life of a man will experience bitterness throughout his life last.

Therefore, it became necessary for a man to suffer for want and needs in his life sometimes to make things right. This is the way by which God can redeem a man for the purpose by which He created man to be.

The purpose of life is now subjected to hardships or circumstances for a man to make right choice with carefulness. For us to be necessary and needful for God's work, circumstances must be permitted by Him to refine man.

This is the solution by which God allow for us to seek Him and to make our friendship regain it stands. Else, man will not have or think that he needs God help through his life due to sin condition he has encountered.

So, God took Abraham and his children to teach the entire world or people the purpose of life and His intention towards them. He led Israel to be a slave in Egypt and then again brought him to His choice of land.

God led Israel in wilderness for forty years to teach the entire world the proper way of life and its purpose. Israel became the subject of proper life sign by which everyman must live.

Israel was allowed to pass through wilderness for forty years with hunger and hardships to regain proper life lost at the beginning.

Everyone must know the life and how it must be live. The object of life is to be regained by man through hardships and circumstances.

Hardship is the rope or messenger that connects us to God or reminds us to seek Him for help. Without this, a man will forever seek things of the world which nothing will prompt him to seek God.

The hardships prompt us to seek God and then to make us strong in doing. In the Christian world and life, God allow circumstances to maintain our relationship to Him then to make us understand the life value.

The journey of Israelites in the wilderness for forty years; is the journey for every Christian. Let every Christian take note of that, without hardship, there will be no good fruit expecting from the tree will be met.

The presence of sin has lost the right choice of a man by which he can be redeemed. We need to experience proper condition of life to make us alive again through hardships.

Let us learn something from the Israelites through their wilderness life and then to understand our Christian life whiles we are journey towards Heaven.

2. Why forty years in wilderness?

Yes, it must be forty years due to the behavior of the Israelites towards their promise land. Their faith was weak. The time of life on earth for human beings was prepared beforehand.

So, it is in every life, it must meet proper preparation before settlement. They were not ready for that precious journey. Yet they needed deliverance from their bondage on where they were. But they were not properly prepared for that journey.

Why they were not ready for that journey? They were seeking for freedom from hardship but not the transformation of their character. They needed freedom from bondage of flesh suffering but not the freedom of God which terminates the sin burden.

As human beings, we love to sit in the comfort zones of sin than to suffer for good life without sin. We cherish freedom from hardship than freedom from sin burden.

Their journey took long years instead of short days. It is because of disobedience. Our way of life is contrary to the principles and order.

In order to be able to inherit the good land, we need to have good character and behavior to possess that land of fruitfulness. Else, we will destroy the beauty of that good land and it productivity.

Many of the Israelites loved the world goods and it abundant. They were satisfied with food, meats and other things but not repentance of bad attitudes.

So, they needed to be train with correct measurement of life matters to be able to inherit the good land promised by God. So, God took them through the series of life, to achieve good character for proper living as wish by Him.

They resisted of been correction and blocked from repentances. The journey to the Promised Land was not just any journey made by man. It is about eternal life and with proper life behavior.

They were subjected to difficulties to be purified by circumstances. They were the cause of that delay, because they were not ready for that freedom.

Sometimes our freedom of life and its best results delaying emanates by lack of readiness and reluctances.

It took forty years for Israelites to reach on the Promised Land; concerning the matters of world loving.

The world matters cannot be carrying towards our journey to the Promised Land. The heart and mind must be clean from unrighteousness and other world matters that kill the soul.

Many people are seeking the best life but failed to practices right principles. This is the cause of Israelites many years in the wilderness. They failed of correction and good attitude, yet wish for life success.

The life matters are the life training tools which no one can avoid and then succeed. As it is difficult to turn water or exchange for oil; so you cannot exchange principles of life to achieve success.

As we are heading towards the Promised Land, we need to obey the rules concerning that. Until we are not ready to change from our sins, the years to reach the Promised Land will be many or prolong.

As Christians, we need to change or repent from unrighteousness and then allow God to lead us through.

We are at the borders of the Promised Land and have spent a lot of time on the wilderness. Let us arise and possess the land.

3. What is the lesson?

The world is the lesson field which involves so many subjects and objects. We are subjected with so many lessons and the reasons to live in the world. The question is why?

There are so many penalties and problems in the world. Evil spirits are all over the world fighting against us physically and spiritually. They are the sources of the world problems and a wreck of human's life.

We are in danger in every moment which needs consideration of act we expose at each day. The journey of Israelites in the wilderness for forty years was an example for Christian's journey to Heaven today.

It is a journey of war against principalities and the forces of darkness. Whatever happened to them will happening to us through this journey we are in today.

Their test at that time is our test today which signifies the beauty of this journey. Our life is dear to God and He wishes our best of life. It is His wish to make us dear again.

Whatever comes our way is His permission for our progress. He loves us and wishes us best and great future. We should not get annoyed when we hate by any danger.

Yet all things work together for our good and progress. The circumstances in our life are our guides which make us strong through this journey of life and its best.

It is the food that sustains the life growth for the best gains. It is not there to harm or kill us, but to boost us and opens our eyes for best steps making. The lessons of life are the teachers of life and the knowledge that gives us correct understanding through our life journey.

The heat that you are passing through will not burns you, but yet to let the sins go and then free you for pure growth that the King demands. We are to achieve best reward which is the life gold that suits the highest stage.

We need to learn more from this life as did Israelites walked in the wilderness for forty years. Whoever wishes to be a Heaven representative will face terrible trials on this earth.

This is not the destiny of the saints but for purification of the character that fits the Heaven one. Our life on this earth has encountered so many stains of sins and it needs to be purifying by circumstances.

Many of us mind has been bought by food and money. This attitude cannot meet the requirements that needs on the Promised Land. Some of us are faithless and timid.

Others love food than life. These are the things that prolong the journey to the Promised Land. The new house needs new goods and new stuff for decoration.

The old nature that has encountered so many stains needs to be prepared and dress with the new one to fit the fresh one. The children of Israel faced scarcity of food and water through their journey into the Promised Land.

They were tested concerning that to proof their faith in God the Almighty. Yet many of them failed for lack of faith and then stumble on the way. Sometime many of us think that, the food is all about life. But that is very wrong!

We are not here on this earth because of food, shelter and so on. That is not God's purpose or intention, yet He wants us to be free and then be like Him.

Many of us lack faith and then fear of wants. The life must sometimes face scarcity of things needed for development. If it were not so, no one will fully meet the will of God that brings eternal life.

The world is full of evil spirits fighting against our progress and our eternal life. Mistakes and other circumstances are our chief teachers teaching us on carefulness.

God permit trials to build us strong and then make us on track sometimes. Let us understand that, material things can steal and then make us lost eternally.

The journey made by the children of Israel in the wilderness for forty years is an example of life matters that every correct Christian must face. Our hearts and minds needs to repent from unrighteousness.

We are rebellion children like the Israelites which resulted their long years in the wilderness. So, trials were permit to let them change from their bad behavior.

As Christians, we will face many trials like them, not to harm us but to bring us on track. We should not worry as the strange thing that has happened to us.

Yet, we must take heart and then be at peace. The promise for us is, I will not leave you nor forsake you! Let us note that, our life is dear to God and He wants us to be like Him and then live with Him.

4. What must you know?

Life is not about money that we seek for each day. It is not like gold that we refine for precious things. Yet, it is a daily practice that needs improvement throughout eternity.

The activities and the actions are the witnesses about the good or bad life we demonstrate each day. What must you know concerning the eternal life? Life is everything concerning world we live.

When life is out, then there is no world or reality. If there is something that needs first and bigger consideration, it is life! The only need that man must seek is life.

As human beings, we must put everything aside and then seek for life first. How must we seek for this life I am talking about? In Him was a life and the life was the light of a man.

He is the resurrection and the life. He is the way, the truth and the life. Many of us are seeking for the properties of the world. Others are seeking for luxuries of this world.

What is the benefit of these things when there is no life? Can you seek for food when you do not have life? Why are you seeking for dead thing instead of life thing? As you cannot build a house without proper preparation, so you cannot make life without life source.

The children of Israel seek for food instead of life and good character. We cannot live without the life giver. So, we must live the life with the life giver.

Everyone must seek the life and it giver before anything else concerning that. We fail of correct attitude as human beings because of sinful nature we have. Many of the children of Israel died for the lack of faith.

The entire children of Israel who began the journey early died on the wilderness because of rebellion. Life is not about food, clothing and shelter. It is about wellbeing that consists of eternal life.

We must consider our attitude and behavior in our entire move. Life is to seek the kingdom of God and it righteousness and all things will be added unto you.

Let everyone consider his or her behavior and then seek for the treasure or pearl of life. The key is that, let all of us seek for the life giver or the master of life. We should avoid those weeds and then seek for the seed. The world and the things in it are for the Lord.

Whatever we see is from Him. Do not let the things of the world take you captive, yet seek the Kingdom of God and it righteousness, then all things will be yours. Means all things will work together for your good.

Let not your heart be trouble, believe in God and move. You cannot always get it right as you wish; but note that, all things will work together for your profit.

In all, mind your business and then fear God! Do not rush and do not do things for granted, else you will fail. The children Israel failed, because of unbelief and distrust.

They thought of flesh, instead of reasoning about their life purpose. Many of them perished in the wilderness and then could not reach the Promised Land. Let us make the most of our time and then keep watch. We will receive the crown. The Israelites were weak in trusting God due to their lack of knowledge about Him. Our life needs knowledge about God than food and shelter which we always seek.

So, God want to us seek Him first in all things. That is why He permits things difficult to our understanding for us to learn and then seek Him for help.

We are the victims of lifelong slavery; lack of proper training and degraded. We need training and knowledge about Him for our progress that fulfill His Standard.

Bless are the pure in heart, for they will see God. Our hearts needs to be purified and train for the purpose of God that fit Him. For us to be with Him for eternity, we need to meet the standard that fit His standard.

The journey of Israelites in the wilderness was not just a journey for freedom of their lives that fit the flesh, but it is the journey that needs to fit God's character. That is the wish of God about our lives.

5. Israel at the red sea

Oh! Can you imagine the big cloud of people moving into their destination together? What lesson can you take from it? Why such a mass of people together moving into their destination? Is there any reason? What has happened?

The children of Israel were led into wilderness instead of passing through the lands of philistines.

It is the direction of God to lead them there. Their way to the Promised Land was to take them about two weeks, in terms of making straight journey as the journey of that area demand.

But God did not lead them on that straight path. Why is it so? What is the purpose? The Bible makes it clear that it is God who led them that way. Why so?

The children of Israel have heard about their Father's God, but they haven't experienced Him before. It is God intention for them to experience Him or know Him well before settle them.

So, He diverted their short days of that journey into long years. Two people agree and then move together.

The children of Israel had no experience with God, yet they had heard about Him before. It is God wish to teach them the matters concerning Himself and then to let them know the works and the character of Himself.

In order to witness about someone, you need to know that person well. It needs long days or years to know someone well. Israel needs to study and then learn about their Father's God and then experience Him and to witness about Him.

So, they were led into wilderness for schooling about God or learn about Him. They were chosen among the nations of the world to be light among them. They are to let the entire nations of the world to know God.

Yet, they need to learn something about God and then experience Him for their mission or witness about Him for chosen them. The children Israel were led to the red sea to learn their first lesson about God greatness.

They were to learn about hope first, when the life seems there is no hope. They must experience their Father's God and to have faith in Him.

Then to know how powerful He is above the god's of Egypt they have encountered. The children of Israel lost their knowledge about God the almighty through their long stay in Egypt.

Their hope as a nation lost in the foreign land concerning their liberty through the long years of stay. The long years in that land of Egypt led them lost their knowledge of God.

Moreover, many of them even forgot the name of the Lord their God. The hope of their liberty got lost through the condition they were in at that time. Their hope became meaningless and out of time. Through long years and hardship led them faithless.

So, their Father's God became their enemy and then hard to trust His word. God intended to let them learn something about Him first and to trust Him. Their lost faith must be built not in a day but with years after.

Yet, they were led into wilderness to study and to know Him. They were led into the red sea where there is no way out. How can they cross this big lake with their kids and other young ones?

Why God did this? Leading many people into where they cannot find way out into their destination.

To God, everything is possible! He can do above what we think or ask concerning all matters of life. Israel was to learn something about Him, who is leading them.

Their faith must be built through circumstances and their lost hope must be established. For them faith is nothing, because they haven't experience such a wonderful thing before.

Fear led them distrusted their leader Moses and then spoke against his deliverance when they saw Egyptians chasing them. They lost their trust and belief in God who have come for them through this meaningless deliverance.

Their questions was why have you brought us into this wilderness occupy by the red sea which there is no way out? To them it was meaningless liberty, because there was no way out through which they were led into.

Those meaningless things to us are meaningful thing to God. Those things that are hard and distrustful by human beings are mere things to God.

For us to know Him well, He must teach us things that are beyond our understanding. Everyone must experience God in at least one day of his or her life about something wonderful.

The matters of life are the concerns of God to improve human's life. So, the children of Israel must be taught concerning the ways of God and to know how He deals with human beings. They were led to the wilderness to learn the works of God.

Now, it is not what you think or wish to have in life, but God wished your great future and hope of better ends. When things become tough, don't give up, yet look up to God and then wait for Him.

The children of Israel lost hope when they saw the Egyptian heading towards them at the shore of the red sea. They cried, and started complaining about how Moses has deceived them on such a journey they have made.

As Christians, whatever life we are going through has been permitted by God already. It is His wish for us to go through that, purposely for our aid and eternal life. Do not think that, you are been hate by Him.

There will be a time in your life which you will experience that all is gone and there is no hope. You will encounter the heat of life that you will be even call for death.

You will regret been on earth and overwhelming that there is no hope for surviving. Yet, do not kill yourself, it shall be well. It is for your good that is why it has come.

Now, Israelites have come to the red sea where there was no way out. Their hope failure when they saw Egyptians coming after them. They thought their life is coming to an end. It is a tough moment for them and where are they going to escape from their enemies? To them, it is now end.

They are about to die without hope; that is their thought. He, who created you, is on your side waiting to hear your voice calling Him.

Will God leave His children to suffer for severe want and die? Will He leave His children for their enemies to perish them?

Does He care? Why frustrations now in my life threaten me? Is there any reason for your negative days and hardships? Why is it so heavy to carry? What is the reason?

Our way of life is very dear to God. Sin has changed our condition which response to God's idea for our progress. Our understanding has been hurt by sin.

In order for us inherit the Kingdom of God; our nature must suit the behavior of God. Everyone who has been called by God must experience His power and nature.

Those people must be purge by circumstances to fit them for eternal land that dwells righteousness. So, the children of Israel were to go through this kind of life before entering the holy land. Whatever our condition as Christians, we must thank God and then accept that condition. Whatever way He lead us, will end in prosperity. Let us consider our ways and doings; then fit us for eternal home.

Our nature and character today cannot inherit the new Heaven and the new earth which dwells righteousness.

Yet, we need to be purifying for the purpose of entering in the holy land. This is way God wanted to lead Israel; for them to fit on their promised land.

It is also our duty to know and experience the power of God. The long journey made by Israel, was to learn and experience the beauty; the power and the mighty works of God. At last the red sea was divided for them to pass through. God will make the way when it seems there is no way.

Then to trust Him and to know who He is! The ways of God are not our ways; the thoughts of God are not our thoughts. As the Heaven is higher than the earth, so the ways; the thoughts of God are higher than us. Whatever way He leads, ends in victory.

6. Why circumstances?

Circumstances are the guides of life which awaking the person or the soul from been wreck by the world matters that fails better life.

It is better for everyone to face some challenge in life; else the person will not learn anything or will fail of proper management.

It opens our eyes and then builds us for good standing. Life is not like running water which goes smooth. It must face some challenges for it to be better live.

Everyone must note that, without challenge or trials, the life cannot be properly managed. All things work together for our good by the purpose of God.

We are in the world of troubles which needs daily guides and proper management. There are lots which we must learn and then take note off. Every day brings new things and then leaves us history which can be learned later by our children who are not yet born.

We need to fight day and night to make the life on it way. No one knows which hour or day will be a bad storm. We all need to prepare and then wait and watch.

The world is running out, things are not as it was at the beginning. There are so many changes and things are deteriorating day and night. There are many cries going on, fears of wants have covered many peoples mind.

It is because so many people love the world and its goods. There must be circumstances that can alert us from slumber. So, circumstance build and bring us back on track.

Our situation as human beings lack responding to righteousness of life. As it is, there is no way that Ethiopian can change his or her burn body. This is our situation as human beings; there is no way that we can change our sinful heart.

We need God intervention to have this change of heart. Concerning this state of ourselves, it is difficult for us to do well or respond to God law which maintains proper life.

So, He (God) permits trials on our ways for us to remember Him in these times of troubles. Then to seek help from Him and to move, else, no one will recognition of Him.

This is our condition when sin comes in our ways. The children Israel desert walk is the best example for us to know the disciplines of God.

As we journey towards the Promised Land, we will face many troubles in our ways. It is not to discourage us, yet to make us strong and then to take care.

Our way of life in this earth is very tragedy. Everyone wants to live by his or her wishes. Many people love the world and its matters. The Christians journey to the Heaven is not the matters of world and its agreements.

Yet, it is a reasonable service and renew of mind for proper human aid and good works. In order for us not go astray from the right path, then comes in circumstance to aid us from straying.

Trials are proper life aid that put us on track and then make us strong as Christians. It opens our eyes and then prompts us to seek God. It awaking us from sleeps and then makes us examining our ways of life.

It is God wish for us to have eternal life. That is why He permits those trials to keep us on track. God does not hesitate on His promise as some thinks.

Yet He has patience for us to come to repentance and does not want us to perish, but to have everlasting life. This is the way sometimes God lead us to be alert and be strong of our daily life.

The lessons of life are the teachers teaching us to take care in our entire move. We are to be strong and enthusiast in all our doings.

So, trials are key guides, which awake us from deviating. The journey of the children of Israel in the wilderness is an example for us as Christians today in our daily life.

The matters we come across at in our daily life are the lessons of our journey towards the promise land. Our daily life must come out with good report and records, which will be a witness for our position each one deserve.

We should not worry about the hardship that comes in but we must focus on the reward or the price. Trials are the efficacies that maintain the better growth of Christian's life standard demand wishes.

So, it is not God intention to kill or makes us worried in our daily life, but to help us fit into our position which He has setup.

The circumstance that comes into our way is the benefit of our life journey that suits the call. Let us consider our doings and change our way of life.

7. I cannot walk alone

Oh how can I live without you and go without your presence? I cannot; dare, walk alone. I need you every day oh precious savior. It is your voice that gives me peace.

My hope is within you and my happiness is to see your face. Please, do not leave me alone and do not turn your eyes from me. My hope is within you. Oh Lord! I cannot go without you or seeing you beside me.

The world is dark and fear allover; I cannot see ahead, shadows across the sky, thunder and lightning are sounding like the waves of sea. Oh Lord! I cannot go without you, walk with me.

Hold my weak hand and lead me on my way. Show me the way I should go and lead me to the end. I cannot; dare, walk alone, Lord Walk with me.

My life is not certain; I cannot see ahead, it seems I am very late than everyone on earth. Oh Lord! It is not late for you, do something and give me strength to hope for. Walk with me. Many things are fighting against me; I cannot move without you Lord, walk with me. In fact, you cannot do without God; neither can you go without Him. Though, your life seems negative; as if all things were against you.

You do not know what to do and do not know where to go. It is hard for you to survive and worse for you to tell your story. There are many things that fighting against you.

Your troubles are filled up and worse things always happen to you. It is not your fight; you cannot do anything about it. Leave to God and be at peace.

For you cannot; dare, fight alone. Let Him fight for you. It shall be well. It is not your duty to fight for your own, but it is your duty to trust and obey His word. That is, your only security to trust and obey Him.

There is no other way to be happy in Jesus, but only to trust and obey Him. Your life is not yours to plan for it greatness and beauty. But leave everything to God and live as His has instruct you.

All things shall work together for your good according to His purpose for you. You cannot; dare, do for yourself by your own effort. You shall fail and be as nothing.

Your life is in His hand and He can turn it as He wants. You have no control about your life but you can do something according to His will and pleasure to please Him.

Only avoid laziness and do what you can through His grace. He will take care of all and make things easier for you. You cannot; dare, do something without Christ.

He knows the plans He had for you; it is for your greatness and future expectation. Do not force yourself to be rich, nor rash for fame. It is not your duty, but your duty is to follow His step as He leads you. It shall be well.

Do your best and what you can and leave the rest to Him and then says, I have done as you instructed me. Lord it is your turn. Do not leave me alone and I cannot; walk alone.

Do not consider your beauty and greatness in future. But consider God first and all things shall be added for you. You cannot; dare, walk alone. He will be with you until the end of time.

8. The life is tough for me

Though, you have done your best as you can but things are not going well as you wish. You need to be tested by circumstances to see if you are fit to handle things well.

It is tough; it is a lesson for your maturity. You do not see clearly; it is not as you know already. Why things have change suddenly? Is it my sins or my destiny? Why these things? It is hard for me now.

What can I do to come out from all these trials? Why things still the same? There is nothing that has change in my life. Still things are tough for me and I do not know why?

You need to be press and know what you can be used for. In life, lessons are our progress act which makes us who we are and what we can do more imagine.

Our ways are not God ways or our thought His thoughts. He knows us more than we do. He created us and knows what is within us.

Sin has changed our beauty and what we can do. We are like gold; we need to refine by fire, then to be useful for the Master.

Whatever your lesson; makes you great and suits you for good use. Do not be worry when things went wrong. But be alert and know what the master have for you.

Do not guess or think of the outcome but be honest and stay cool until the end. It is for your good but not your wreck. You need to be fit for the position you about to be hold.

It is not what you think but it is His will to make you great and fit for good works. You cannot; dare, do it by your strength. He (God) will do it for you.

It is not your duty to stress yourself about world matters. But it is your duty to seek His kingdom first and then all things will be added for your good. Why is it hard for you? It means you are worthy to do and handle more.

You need to be trained for it and then set you for good works and victory. You cannot; it is tough for you, you wish to give up. You cannot entertain it again. You are tire of your situation.

Do not be afraid; it is for your good but not your ruin. Be faithful to the end; do not allow it for sin. Your trials are your master which teaches you how to hold yourself for great things.

It is not for wreck but your fame. Let it not be a strange thing happens to you. But keep in mind that all things work good for God's people that are called be His purpose.

Leave everything to Him and be at peace; why are you challenging? You have something special to do for God and His people around you. It is you only that you can do that thing.

So, you must be trained for and make things well to suit the Master wishes. He will not leave you alone do by your strength. He has prepared the way you should do it with ease.

You will not get as you wish, but you will get it as God wishes. Without Him you can do nothing. You must be train for; else you will do foolish things which will lead you into destruction.

It is for your good that it has come so. In fact, my dear your life is not in your hands to make it as you wish. It is in the hands of God.

Whatever transpires has a purpose for your life. It is for good and great expectation but not for your ruin. Keep it in mind and be honest to the end.

9. Without you I can do nothing

How can I do without you oh Lord? How can I go without you? I will lose; if I dare, Lord holds me firmly in this trouble world. What can I do Lord apart from you?

I cannot live without you and I cannot go without you. My ways are evil all day long. I am weak; I need your hands to support me. What can I do, that will appreciate you? My good works are like rag before you.

My ways are wrong and my doings are pretense. What can benefit me without you? Only you can do through me for your own appreciation. Our doings are always evil and our ways are trick.

We cannot do to appreciate God, unless He does through us. Never think you without God or Christ. Our Life and ways are for Him and the world and everything in them are for Him.

He owns everything and through Him all things were made. In Him that we move and have our beings; He is our maker and savior. It is His will that we were created. In fact, we cannot live without God as human beings. Everyone must note that, without Christ; he or she is nothing. Apart from Him, we are nothing and cannot be counted as anything. Who are you and what can you do? He is the true vine and we are His branches.

Whatever the branch can do must come from the vine itself. The breaches have no root but it depend on the vine to survive. When one of the breaches avoids the vine feed, it will collapse and then die.

This is how we live and move through our maker. If we avoid Him, we avoid life and wish to cease forever. You cannot do or live without Him. He is our source of life and everything we need.

Maybe you may try with your own effort, but what will be the end. It is even impossible for you to do without God. You should worry yourself anything, but leave to God and be at peace.

It shall be well and without Him, you can do nothing. Many people want to do great things by their own strength. But what will be the results? Do not think that you can do by your own might. It is not so, you cannot, except He (God) allows it.

Else, it will avian in nothing. So, we are nothing without God and cannot be anything apart from Him. You should not boast on things that you have been able to do.

It is not by your strength; your wise or your ability. But it is by His grace that made that chance for you to do. You do not have any idea and do not own anything concerning your skills. You cannot without Him do something.

It is by the grace that He provides and then makes us do and move. It is His depth of mercy that we as sinners move and live. We have nothing to do about it.

He is our life and creator. He wants us good and wishes our best. It is not by your ability or strength, but it is His mercy and grace. I cannot do without you, Lord! Hold my hands and lead me. Without you; I will be nothing and cannot do for myself. It is only you can do through me. I cannot; dare, do without you! Please, do not leave me, be my guide and helper. I cannot; dare, do without you.

10. My life is yours

Oh Lord! Do not leave me, I am your son and my life is yours. It is now finished; my hope is gone. What will happen to me? Please, do not leave me; my life is yours.

It is now destroy; how can I get it back? My eyes is upon you; it is only you can do. My life is yours. Many people are seeking my fall and disgrace. My hope is gone; it is only you can do.

Please, do not leave me, my life is yours. I have wasted my time for nothing and people are laughing at me. What should I do? I am getting old and nothing shows my progress.

Only you can do. Please, do not abandon me, my life is yours. It is so that your life is not certain and it is seems it has ended. There is nothing show that you will be somebody at the end.

You have spent your time for nothing. But it is not late yet. There is hope for the hopeless. Let your pray be my life is yours; Lord do not leave but have mercy on me.

Your life must be certain in God but no other. The world has nothing for you. He can do beyond what you think or ask, it is not yet your time.

But keep waiting and waiting. Do not destroy your beauty by bribe or any enticement. Only be faithful and do what you can.

Make your life His life; means surrender everything to Him and wait for His time. He will not fail you or forsake you. You cannot; dare, live by your strength and insight. But leave all for Him and take heart.

It is not your duty to worry about your future. But it is your duty to surrender your life to Him, and then do what you can and comfort yourself. It is shall be abundantly well. To you there is no hope, but to Him (God) all things are possible.

It is not yet late but it is a beginning of your life before God. He is going to start everything fresh in your life and those who are laughing at you, will be shock and ashamed.

Live as He wish but not your desire. It is not yet late at all. Only have hope in Him or trust Him. God is deeply willing to do everything for you. He is ever ready to welcome and comforted.

Do not think that your problem is not His problem or He does not mind. He is just watching that, if you will mind as He is and then reward you who seek Him.

Consider and only say; let my life be dear to you, oh precious savior. Keep near to me and hold my hands.

I cannot; dare, live my life, my life is yours. Control everything about me and let me hope you care. My life is yours. I heard your voice calling me to come and have rest.

I have come; give me rest as your voice is saying. I cannot; dare, do for myself, Please give me rest.

You are my hope; my shield and my redeemer. It is for you to act; my heart is breaking, my hope is in you, oh precious savior, I come to you.

If the world turns around and hope lost; my life is yours, Please Lord, do not leave, I cannot; dare, move without you. My life is yours. It is good that you press me.

Now I have seen what I can do for you. It is not my wish but by your wish, help me do according to your instruction and then do it right.

My life is yours. I know you have learnt a lot and pray as well. What is your aim now and what do you want to do for Him? Is your life is His?

11. Hold me; I am weak

In fact, I cannot do for myself and I do not know how to do it. It is not my fault; I do not know how I must do it. I cannot; I cannot do for myself. I am weak and you are strong, please do it for me.

How will I live my life, if you leave me alone? It is difficult for me to move around; when I see your absences.

Sometimes I feel your absence and thought you have left me alone. I will make a mistake, if you leave me a moment.

It is tough for me to go, when I feel your absence. Why have you forsake me; Lord? My enemies are all over, wanting to find fault on me.

I do not understand my weakness. I always wrong, when I want to do right. I cannot do for myself; unless you do for me. How can I dare, do for myself? Hold me please; I am weak.

When I am listening; I wrong, when I am writing I make mistake, when I am walking, I flop and find fault when I am looking. Who will rescue me from this weakness? It is only you; Lord. Hold me; I am weak. I cannot; dare, walk alone, please, do not leave me.

It is not my fault, I do not understand; please hold me, I am weak. I cannot push; I do not know how to control myself. Please, hold me, I am weak.

I am fast to do wrong than good and wish flesh than the spirit. That is, my nature; I do not know why it is so with me? I consider nothing, unless I wrong in doing.

Please, hold me, I am weak. Your condition is not problem to God. Though, you are the worse sinner on the earth. His word to is come and let us reason together.

It is not late and your sin is ordinary before His grace. He can forgive the sin above sin, only if you will accept you're wrong and confess before Him. He is faithful to give all your sins and then cleanse you from it.

It does not matter your weakness or your sins that you been committed. God is able to forgive you by accepting and confess it to

Him. He will not leave you to struggle alone and will not hide His face from you. Only recognize Him as your Lord and savior. He cares and mind than His apples of His eyes. You are dear to Him and will not forsake you.

Be not afraid to come to Him. He is merciful to forgive your sins and then cleanse you from all unrighteousness. You cannot live by your strength.

You will fail and be as nothing. Do not allow perplexities overcome you. You I cannot; dare, control the forces around the globe. Only allow His to rule and guide.

Your life cannot be accepted by God. If you dare, live by your own strength. It is not you but it is Him who works in us to His good pressure and what pleases Him.

For by grace we have been saving, not by works, and then anyone should boast. You always need Christ to lead you. He is presence each minute to help and rescue sinners.

He is calling you with His tender voice; He is calling, He is calling, oh sinner come home. The beauty of His calling is that, He does not demand anything from you.

Your duty is to accept His voice and then go as He is calling you. Though, you are weak, but His grace is abundant for your weakness. Hold me; please, I am weak. Only accept it this way, He will accept you and then forgive you.

12. It is now dark in my life

What I am now seeing? So, this is how life is? It is now dark in my life. Sometimes life becomes worse and beyond compare. You always fail when you try.

You have attempted twice but you fail. It is now the third one but you cannot see it well. You ask yourself why? You do not understand the reason why you always when you want to do something.

It cannot go well with you. You ask yourself why and why? Why me? You always fail, when you want to do. You start and it fall, no I cannot understand, no I cannot understand.

I will look into it, no, I will look into it. What can you do? Do you know the reason? Do you know what is going to happen, when you dare? It is dark in your life; yes, it is dark but do you know why?

There is nothing that will happen that has no reason. It is a reason and it is for the purpose. Who knows the end of each one's life?

Who can tell the reason of such incidences that comes to life of each individual? Who knows the answer and who can tell reason?

Darkness in life has reason and the purpose it serves. In this world, there is a night with a day.

The night serves as resting time for all human beings and it fit us for the day activities which are before us. So, it is in life, darkness time fit us for day time activities and keeps us fit continuously.

When your life turns around and things are not going well, do not be afraid, it is for your aid fitting you for future duty.

This should not be a new thing but it is giving you a lesson for future progress and wellbeing. It is dark in your life; you cannot, dare, solve by your own strength.

It is for a reason and letting you on something necessary for you improvement. Do not, dare, make a mistake in trying times; Else, you will lost the purpose by which you been called to do.

If you dare, you will fail the Master. You cannot; dare, do something about it. Leave to God and be at peace.

Darkness hours are experience time that will build you for good work and great glory in the near future of your life. It is not yet over but it is a lesson time.

Do not think that it is gone and nothing can be done about it. Life is not easy as some people take it to be. It is more than a war between two forces of power.

It is needs giants to face and wise to control. But you cannot; dare, make it without God. It is not over but there is hope. You need to consider your doings and manage it to the due time. It has an end, it will not last.

Do not fear and be discouraged. Do not say it is me again but give thanks to God and be at peace. You cannot do something about it but wait for God and have hope in Him.

It is not yet over. Let your prayer be oh Lord Fight for me, I cannot; dare, fight. This fight is for you but not me.

Please, fight for yourself and do not include me. It is your fight but not mine. Everyone have duty and purpose to achieve in this earth.

Sin has caused a lot to count with; many things have change and our life have question and to be solve. Though, it is now dark in your life but it is not permanent; it will cease, Hope in God, it shall be well.

13. Show me the way

Lord I come to you just I am; I need your mercy and grace. Do not turn your eyes from me. I am yours, I cannot; dare, be alone. I am in dark in this state of my life.

I have go far end in my life. I am over age; I am getting old and my way is now end to do. I do not know what to do and where to go. Oh Lord, show me the way I should go.

I do not know where I should go and I not know the way forward. I see dark before me, I cannot go forward and I cannot come back. So, this is how it is in life? I do not know that is life beyond estimation.

Jesus savior pilots me on these waves of life. You are the pilot on the sea which rows and waves here and there. I cannot; dare, go alone without your presence. It is even tough to me to move on these waves of life.

How can I dare, go without you? Jesus savior shows me the way. The life is hard for me and I have spent my time without improvement.

To me, there is no way out, you are the pilot of life, Jesus savior pilots me. I have come to the place where the waves are so strong to pass through, and I cannot go forward again, oh Lord Jesus, please hold my hands and lead me.

To me it is end, but to you it is now beginning; Precious savior pilots me. Loving shepherd protect your sheep, your power is stronger than every power. Please protect me from those enemies who are seeking my life.

The life is tough for me to live. I look to you, though my life is almost end and my hope is gone but you are strong and mighty to do. Please make it your own and rescue me from these troubles.

Show me the way; I am lost and have mixed my target. Nothing is late for you, please favor me and then settle my case. Jesus guide my way and lead me to home. That is, I need your comfort and grace in my life.

The way is dark for me to move on; I cannot step forward, please I look to you and waiting. I cannot; dare, go without you, my hope is gone. Please, lead me home. It is fact that all your hope is gone. There is nothing left; to you the life has ended. It is true that you are suffering and all hopes are gone.

Do not be afraid, it is not waste yet. If you have life; you have hope, it is not late yet. Your time is coming and you shall forget all your troubles and sufferings.

Only trust Him; He who create you. He will show you the way that you should go. Whether it is left or right, when you pass on it, it shall be well with you. It is yet waste but it is now beginning.

Thirst and see that, God is good, for those who run to Him are saved. It is not yet late at all.

Have hope and live according to His wish, and all will be added to you. Oh shepherd of tender youth lead me on my way.

Let this be your prayer every day and keep on and keeping on. The mountains that you see always before you shall vanish and you will be set free and have your peace.

God is ever ready to help and rescue us from our troubles. He loves the world and wishes the world life and progress. Woman can forget her child who she has given birth to, but God will not forget us even in the moment.

He cares and shall show you the way you should go. Keep these messages and think about it day and night.

14. Do not leave me, Please!

It is still dark, nothing has change; I am now afraid. It seems I am about to die. Do not leave me, please! I cannot; dare, sleep alone.

It is now day, everyone is going to his or her job. But my job has broken and do not know where to turn.

Do not leave me, please, I cannot; dare, be at home alone. It is far beyond my understanding, this life is hard for me, and I cannot hold it. Do not leave me, please, be my help.

I have struggle a lot but it is not okay for me. I am tire and I cannot continue again. Do not leave me, please, I cannot; dare, continue without you. It has overcome me and I am dying. Please, do not leave me, I cannot; dare, keep on.

I need you Lord and I cannot be alone without you. Come near to me and comfort me. Abide with me; night is fast falling, now I see darkness all over, I am afraid Lord abide with me. I need you every minute, please, do not leave me.

Be my friend and sit beside me, my heart is paining me. I cannot sit or sleep without you. Do not leave me, please! I cannot; dare, be alone.

You are the friend in deed; your love is beauty. You have answered me. Now my heart is cheer. You have comfort me and have given me hope. Your name be the glory.

You always near when I call and always comfort when I am afraid. Oh Lord your love is kind and beautiful. My hope is in you, you are my shelter and protector. You love beauty and wish your children's well.

You know the thought that you are thinking towards us. It is not of evil but of peace and great hope. You love the world and gave your only son our salvation.

We are grateful for that precious act. It is enough and nothing can be compared with. It is deeper than love itself and difficult to understand. You love man than yourself; it is very wonderful and great.

Who can understand your doing and know your ways. It is higher than the highest and bigger than the biggest. God love us no matter our condition as human beings.

He can forgive every sin that we have committed and then cleanse us from all unrighteousness. Your life is in His hand and He always remembered us.

He says do not be afraid or discourage. I will be with you to the end of age. I will not leave alone; you are mine until your old age I will carry you on my shoulders.

He knows you from the womb of your mother and has set you to be his prophet for the nations.

To pull down and rebuilt, you are His apples of His eyes love and protected. It is not His will to suffer you for want but it is for your aid and future greatness.

He does not want you to perish but come to repentance. He will not leave you or forsake you, you are dear to Him. He valued your life and wishes your life than death.

He always considers your suffering and takes note of it. He mind and always welcome you. Let's read Isaiah 43:1-7; read;

But now, thus says the LORD, who created you, O Jacob, And He who formed you, O Israel: "Fear not, for I have redeemed you; I have called you by your name; You are Mine.

2When you pass through the waters, I will be with you; And through the rivers, they shall not overflow you. When you walk through the fire, you shall not be burned, nor shall the flame scorch you.

3For I am the LORD your God, The Holy One of Israel, your Savior; I gave Egypt for your ransom, Ethiopia and Seba in your place.

4Since you were precious in my sight, you have been honored, And I have loved you; therefore I will give men for you, and people for your life.

5Fear not, for I am with you; I will bring your descendants from the east, and gather you from the west;

6I will say to the north, "give them up!' And to the south, "do not keep them back!' Bring my sons from afar, and My daughters from the ends of the earth—

7Everyone who is called by my name, whom I have created for my glory; I have formed him, yes, I have made him."

God is aware of our situations and there is nothing that comes without His permission. He will not leave us to suffer for our own but He will rescue and build us for new beginnings.

Let your prayer be; Oh Lord; do not leave me and I cannot; dare, walk alone. Take my wish and live my life for me. It is yours, make it just as you want and be my guide always. I cannot; dare, live my life; please live it for me, for my life is yours.

Show me the way I should go, I cannot; dare, walk alone. Never think it is all gone or be discouraged because of waves you see.

It shall stop and peace will be still. It is late, but you I cannot; dare, walk alone. Let God lead, it shall be completely well. It is your time; be comfort and keep watch!

15. Are you troubled?

Have you lost hope? What's your problem? Is there any hope for you? Yes! Do not be afraid and do not lose heart.

What will be my end? Oh, my hope is gone. How can I find way out? When shall I come out from this problem?

Oh, it is finished. These are your questions day and night. When will this situation change? I am tired, I cannot go forward again. Many things fight against our progress and there is nothing that you can do by your power.

If you dare, you shall fail and be as nothing. Never lose hope but be at peace and then leave everything to God. To you, everything has destroyed but to God, it is well and fresh for your progress.

Do not give up but keep mind that you should be in that situation and it is for a purpose that you are in that condition. Life penalties are life success and it is better to hurt your leg by stone than to go without any hurt. Note; without a lesson, there is no knowledge or formation for awareness. You need to go through lessons and then have knowledge for improvement.

We all need experience for better life and improvement. If you are going through problems, do not take it a curse or wrecks of your life. But it teaches you to be on top at the end.

Troubles are the teachers of a better life that makes you achieve lasting belongings. God allows circumstance to build us for good work and future expectation.

Your troubles are your teachers guiding you to prove self-esteem. Without life lessons, you cannot live a worthy life. Your Lessons will prove your inner beauty and then prepares you for greater responsibilities.

It is for purpose and the reasons why you have come into that situation. Do not worry when you are in trouble, but always thank God for that situation.

He who sees you know what is within you and what you can do for Him. It is for a reason; you must take note of that, and then accept it in good faith.

He will not leave you or forsake you to struggle with what you cannot overcome. He is aware and has allowed it for your good but not your ruin. Listen to His words; come to me, he who is labor and with heavy laden, I will give you rest.

You need to have patience and hope of your condition. You need to learn something, that why you are in that situation.

You must learn that. You must take that lesson or condition seriously; else you will fail and then disappoint your Master who allows it.

You are gold and you are precious for the Master. So, you should go through fire to be purged for good use.

There is something within you that is needed, and that thing needs to come out through fire.

Your situation is not doom but for a reason, that will let others know the inner beauty of you and how useful you are. Your problems are your aid builds you to do excellent work in future for God.

He knows the plans He has for you, not the broken ones but fit ones necessary for others aid and your future hope. Do not be troubled, it is for your good.

16. What are you looking for?

The world has abundant of things and the purpose of those things. Though, everyone has his or her needs but what is the benefit of those needs?

In all, what will be the end of those wants? What are you looking for? Why are you looking for that thing?

Do those things have something important for you? There is something you should know that supersedes your needs. I know that what you are seeking for is important to you. But there is something important than what are looking for.

We all have a direction that we are heading towards. Everyone has something before him. But what will be the outcome?

Oh, why are you seeking for weeds instead of seed? Why are you seeking for sand instead of gold?

Why are you seeking for dust instead of food? Many people have put aside the great object of life. Others too are seeking for food instead of life.

Many of them do not have any object before them, but living aimlessly. You should not disturb yourself of things that do not have any benefit for the soul.

But you must seek first the kingdom of God and His righteousness and all things will be added onto you.

We need not worry about our lives on what we will eat and cloth. Though it is needed that should not be our priority. He who created us knows our needs and worries and knows what is first and best for our souls.

We must seek first His kingdom and His righteousness. This should be the first and priority of our being. This life is not for us to carry the burdens into ourselves. But we should leave everything to Him who created us.

He will take care of them and then provide the necessary thing in due time for us. It is not your duty to carry those burdens into yourself. But you have to let Him known by prayer and He shall provide for you abundantly above what you think or ask.

It is time to let God know your needs and problems. Do not worry about time or when your problems will be solved. Yet, let Him know your needs by seeking first His kingdom.

God loves to hear your voice. He does know your problems, but He wishes to hear your voice. You are dear to Him and wish to have you.

If you know what God can do for you, then you will not worry yourself of the things that are passing out. You need to have patience; trust and obey Him.

You must consider your words and your actions towards your daily activities. Do not abuse yourself on wants but be patient and wait for due time. Matters of life are matters of wants and needs.

But the only thing that will help us most is to seek first God's kingdom and His righteousness, and then all things will be added onto us.

You must look for gold not dust; you must seek for food that will earn you everlasting life not the temporal. Seek life but not vanity and seek eternal goods, but not the wind.

17. Are you wondering?

Sometimes life becomes hard and difficult to live. What shall I do about my situation? Where should I go to have relief? I do not know what to do? Can I survive in this condition?

These are your questions concerning your situation. But what have you observed about these conditions? Note: in all, you are still alive; you have not died yet. Have you asked that, why you are still alive?

Your circumstances and trials are your teachers guiding you to succeed. It is not there to destroy you, but it is building you to stand firmly.

In fact, bad conditions do not come to kill, but to make you alert and then prepares you for good management.

Do not wonder why it has happened to you. But learn to behave well in it. A calamity comes to prepare us for good works but not to wreck us.

Every bad situation has a purpose for us as human beings. Our condition has changed because of sin. So, it is good for us to suffer and to make a change.

Do not wonder why? But ask for the reason and then make a change. Do not lose hope, stop doubting and be at peace. It is not your doom but it is your welfare and correction.

Your life is not yours to make it the way you want it. But it is a choice and how you want by choice. One thing you should know is that it is God who directs your path and ends with your commitment.

Do not be afraid and never be discouraged. He knows the plans He has for you and thoughts that will make your success. Do not wonder or doubt about your situation.

He, who created the heavens and the earth, knows what are the best and good for you. He cares and shall not leave you alone to wonder. He, (God) allows trying times to come upon us and prepare us for good works.

It is not your duty to direct your path but you must allow God to direct it for you. You need to consider why you are still alive with all poverty and hopelessness situation.

This means that you are loved and accepted by God. Be happy in all your condition, whether good or bad. Leave everything to God and stay at ease.

Your life is dear to Him and He will let you live in all your trials. God has seen you wondering, He is aware of that, He will do something about it. You should not stress yourself in the condition you cannot do anything about it.

Do not speculate, else you shall possibly lose your life. But be hopeful and knows that He (God) cares.

This world was created for you, and you are the manager of those things that are in. what else do you need that is absent?

It is the sin of our first parents that has brought discomfort in life. But in all, it is for our aid and good to be in discomfort.

Do not wonder; it is there for a moment, it shall come to pass. Do not think that it is finished and yet there is no hope again.

Be hopeful, it is gone yet, but it is preparing you for your future crown. Are you wondering? Stop and be at peace. It shall be well.

18. Does God care?

Yes! He cares; He waits to see if you shall respect and call Him for help. He keeps on waiting and allows trials to treat you for repentance and salvation. It is not His wish to suffer you wrong but it is for the reason of your life.

Our ways are not God ways, neither our thought His thoughts. As the heavens are higher than the earth, so His thoughts are higher than our thoughts. What can you imagine? What have you thought off?

Look at the lily of the field as Christ mentioned. Look at the birds and other insects. Think of the fishes in the sea.

Do they work? Where do they get their food from? In all, have you consider or observe the termites and ants, where do they get their food?

What have you learnt from all these living things? Who feeds them or care for them? Are you not worthier than them? You, who have little faith; what do you, want? What can you do concerning your life? It is not your duty to stress about how you will be. But you have to leave everything to God.

Can you add one cubic into your height? What can you do to make your life better? Can you build to the sky? Why are you wrecking yourself with unnecessary thoughts?

Never think that God does not care about you. Do not be faithless because of darkness that is now around you.

In fact, you are not alone, no matter what you see and feel. God has noticed your problems and it is He who allows it.

It is not a mistake that you have done. But it is for your aid. Maybe you have done a mistake, have you asked why you made that mistake? It does not matter what you have done wrong, He (God) is still caring for you.

Hagar became disrespectful to her mistress (Sarah) when she saw that she had conceived. She was sack from home and then wandered in the wilderness. She was distress and became hopeless, but God did not leave her to suffer because of her stubbornness. God sent Angel to aid her from suffering and comforted by the Angel.

God has seen your suffering and has taken note of it. He will not leave you or forsake you. He is the God who sees and He has seen your afflictions. He knows everyone and cares for each one of us.

It does not matter your wrongs and mistakes. He cares for you and wishes you well. You are always present in His sight and loved. Do not worry or fear wants. God will not leave us to suffer for wants.

He is near to help and to rescue. Leave your burdens on Him, for He cares for you. Note: Hagar wandered in the wilderness on the second time with her child (Ishmael) and their water was used up.

She thought she was going to lose her son. There was no water for both to drink. Her hope lost and became worried. But God provided water without her knowledge and she was refreshed and then encouraged by the Angel of Lord. What is your problem? Have you lost hope? God is aware; He will take care of it. Do not be afraid, He cares for you!

19. Why all these troubles?

Troubles are pressures that come upon us and it is disturbing to the body and the soul. Why troubles and how does it help us?

Where from it? Have you asked yourself why troubles come in my way? What purpose does it serve?

Troubles make us learn a lot in life matters and then open our way for progress. So, it is good that we come into circumstance sometimes. But it is not always necessary to come into troubles; else you can fail or fall.

In all, troubles build us to stand firmly in life. It is not God's will to lead us into troubles, but He permits it to come sometimes in our lives to aid us to live carefully.

Pressure comes sometimes in our life for our progress. Here, this means no pressure; no progress in our life sometimes.

Circumstances are God workmanship for our progress. That builds us to make a good choice and then open our eyes for greater achievement.

There is nothing come without a purpose in which it came. Our nature needs pressure to progress and knowledge to preserve the beauty of the being.

Sin has damaged our being and there is nothing that can change it unless it passes through circumstances.

So, it is needed to pass through pressure to preserve your soul. The fact is that God allows trials sometimes to come to us and then discipline us through it.

So, when troubles come into your life, never take it as a wreck for your soul, but learn the lesson it has for you and then keep yourself well.

Do not be afraid, yet be considerate and build yourself well. Life without a lesson or experience cannot be a successful life. Your life needs stages and lessons in each stage.

If not, you will not be a good manager. Leaders need the experience to lead those under them. But experience without knowledge destroys the beauty of the leadership.

Many people do not aim high in life; the truth is that they become less at the end. And these people sometimes do not meet circumstances in their life and then have less knowledge.

But those who aim high ideally go through trials and disappointments. Their life sometimes comes worrisome and burden. But these people become leaders and sometimes lead God's people to the Promised Land. Example (Moses)

Those with less experience are easy to become discouraged and easy to lose faith. God sometimes choose those who are poise and truthful in little things for His work. Yet, they are not without fault but will to do just as they are.

Your life needs lesson and knowledge before to be God's priest who shepherds His sheep. Who knows, maybe your troubles are for your leadership in future or shepherd of God's sheep.

Do not take things for granted when you are going through circumstances. But learn the lesson and then keep in mind the reason it came. Is it not a reason that these troubles have come?

It is for a reason and the purpose it serves. So, take heart and be at peace. It is there for your progress and salvation. We need to be discipline in life stages due to our lifelong slavery situations.

20. It shall be well

Now there is darkness around you and your hope is gone. Your life is uncertain; you do not know what to do and does not know what is going to happen to you in the next hour.

Do not give up but be of good courage and hold your peace. Do not mind to move when there is a deep darkness around you. Means do not give up when you meet problems or fail in life.

You cannot get everything smoothly in life as you want it or expected. You shall face a lot of circumstances, but those circumstances are your help. It came for your progress and fame.

You shouldn't let it shout you in but come out with all successfulness. It shall be well, do not fear! The sea waves always move with different energy and it does not rest with a single moment.

It teaches the spirit of consistency in life. This is how everyone must work and move when there is life. Those who have experienced a lot of hardship do not mind the waves of life. You need to keep in mind that, life does not have a limit in which it ends unless you die. Else, you should go forward every day. You should not rest; if you dare, you shall not win the fight as you want it.

You keep on going every day and do all you can to achieve the goal before you. It shall be well. You shall not get it easy; but you need to move forward, you shall win.

The only thing you need to do is to do your part as you can. Do not worry about the problems you are facing and do not dismay but leave everything to God and be at peace.

Keep it in mind that whatever the problem, it shall come to end. Dark days are preparation and learning days for every human being.

The world consists of days and nights and these forms weeks; months and years to make the development of the life of people.

So, dark days are part of life; and it depends on both for the life to become dear. You cannot do away dark days in your life, neither can you do away a night from the light which makes a day.

The life consists of dark and light to develop as the day form part of the night to make a day; so is life.

Everyone must note that life consists of dark and light to be life. Do not be afraid when you face problems and note that it is part of life. No condition is permanent, the dark days shall go and the light days will come. It will never be dark forever; either can it be light forever.

Both work together for your good. It will never be the same as you see it; it will change and shall be well. You cannot enjoy life always, neither can you be in darkness always, but you shall be in both situations for the proper development of your life. That is how God made and you cannot escape or avoid them in life.

Do not be discouraged and do not be afraid of the storms that you see; it is there to assist you for the proper growth of your life and shall not last. You need to renew your strength and set your head up for joy. Note this text; Fear not, for I am with you; be not dismayed, for I am your God. I will strengthen you, Yes, I will help you, I will uphold you with My righteous right hand.' (Isaiah 41:10). Be at peace, it shall be well.

21. He is waiting to hear you

Consider this text, come and let us reason together says the Lord God. He is always waiting to see if you will call Him. He is the God who sees and I have seen Him who sees me.

We are not alone and have not been abandoned by God. He is always waiting to see if we will call Him.

God is waiting to hear from us. He loves to hear our voice and wishing to help us abundantly above what we think or ask.

He cares and always wants to hear our voices. Do not disturb your mind with so many things that are unnecessary for your life, but leave everything to God and be peace. It is time for us to seek God with all our mind and souls.

What God cannot do? What is your problem? What you need to keep in mind is that God always cares, no matter your trials that you are going through. He is always near to help and willing to do above what we imagine.

Sometimes we wonder why things are not going well as want it and think that God has abandoned us.

He has seen all our worries and it is He who allows it to come upon us. He wants us to call Him or communicate our problems to Him. He has a thousand ways to provide for you in which you know nothing.

You cannot do for yourself, you need Him to do for you, and else you shall fail. Some time ago, Jesus and His disciples were in a boat wanted to cross to the other side of the sea and the waves were too heavy on them.

Jesus was asleep on the other side of the boat, the windstorm was heavy and the boat started filling.

The Disciples struggled to find way out but they could not. They forgot that they were with Jesus on the boat. Sometimes waves of life let us forget God who created us. But what can we do if we forget Him?

The Disciples of Jesus at that time struggled with their strength but they could not achieve their goal.

What do you want to do that you are struggling with? Note; the Disciples of Jesus couldn't until they recognize Jesus and called Him.

Then Jesus calms the storms by saying peace be still. The wind ceased and there was a great calm.

They feared exceedingly, and said to one another, "Who is this man, that even the wind and the sea obey Him! You cannot do for yourself by your strength.

You shall fail by your insight, but you will and recognize Him, you shall be free from all the problems you are going through. Only, if you will recognize and call Him. What are your storms? What can you do about it?

He is waiting to hear from you concerning the problems that you are facing. Will you call Him? You must call Him and then hold your peace. What are the reactions of the Disciples?

What did they say? Do you not care that we are perishing? Then He arose and rebuked the wind.

He is waiting to hear your voice and then respond to your needs. Will you call Him? You cannot go forward or move on when you reject Him.

All that you are doing cannot reach anywhere unless you recognize the one who created you. Do not leave God and live your life. If you dare; it will be fruitless.

God knows everything that is going on in our lives, and He is willing to hear from us concerning our difficulties and then solve it permanently for us. Will you approach Him with your problems?

22. Do not be afraid

Are you afraid? Are you discouraged? Do not be afraid? Do not be faithless? Maybe you do not believe God who created the heavens and the earth. It is the greatest sin to distrust God the heaven and creator.

Do not shorten the hands of God through you distrust of His word. What do you know about yourself? Do you know where you come from? If you do not know, then close your mouth. What do know about your life?

What can you do, if you do not know where you come from? Why are you fearful? Can you predict the end of your life? What do you know about the world and the creatures? Who feed the living ones and care for the non-living?

Do you have any idea? What can you say concerning the things of the world? Why are you challenging? Can you add one cubic to your height? Do you provide for the fishes in the sea? What is your burden?

What is weaning you down? Do you know the square meter of the earth? Can you measure the volume of the sea? Do you know the size of it? Did God has asked you to count all trees on the earth for Him? Do you know the density of this earth? Why are you afraid? Who is after you or chasing you? There is nothing to be fear in life and there is nothing that should border you.

Do not be afraid of anything but give thanks to God in all seasons. Do not make God small of your needs or do not short His hand through your disbelieve. You need not worry about anything.

Only let God hear your voice in prayer. He will take care of your problems and then solve them for you. As the child depends on his or her parents, so you should depend on God of your life. You need to trust Him.

Do not be afraid at all. Your problems are His problems. He is willing to provide and cares about your needs. He will not leave you to suffer for hunger. He will pour water on the dry ground and will make stream on the desert.

It is not your duty to be overwhelmed with many things. As you cannot do anything about day and night concerning this life matters.

So, you should stay calm and look to God. He is your provider in time of needs. Note: what Isaiah said concerning God's care for His children.

Read; 2"Enlarge the place of your tent, and let them stretch out the curtains of your dwellings; Do not spare; Lengthen your cords, and strengthen your stakes.

3For you shall expand to the right and to the left, and your descendants will inherit the nations, And make the desolate cities inhabited.

4"Do not fear, for you will not be ashamed; neither be disgraced, for you will not be put to shame; for you will forget the shame of your youth, and will not remember the reproach of your widowhood anymore.

5For your Maker is your husband, The LORD of hosts is His name; and your Redeemer is the Holy One of Israel; He is called the God of the whole earth. (Isaiah 54:2-5)

God is your husband and your redeemer. What is your problem? What He cannot provide for you? Is anything too hard for Him that He cannot do? He owns the Heavens and the earth. He is called the God of the whole earth.

Is there anything that He cannot do? Indeed, He can do all things. There is nothing that cannot worry Him or disturb Him. You need not fear for wants or dismay about anything. Leave everything to Him and take heart. Disturb God by your prayers and let Him see your face every day and then hold your peace. Let nothing discourage you but keep on trust God about His words. He wants to hear your voice and you are dear to Him.

Consider this text; Ho! Everyone who thirsts, Come to the waters; and you who have no money, Come, buy and eat. Yes, come, buy wine and milk Without money and without price.

God is willing to give you anything you need. He will not request anything from you. You shall not pay for what He is giving to you.

It is free. He has seen your troubles and has seen your burdens. He is with you and cares. He is the God who sees and He has seen your trials. Note;

When you pass through the waters, I will be with you; And through the rivers, they shall not overflow you. When you walk through the fire, you shall not be burned, Nor shall the flame scorch you.

For I am the LORD your God, The Holy One of Israel, your Savior; I gave Egypt for your ransom, Ethiopia and Seba in your place.

Since you were precious in My sight, You have been honored, And I have loved you; Therefore I will give men for you, And people for your life. (Isaiah43:2-4)

We are not alone; God is with us. His name is Immanuel. He is with us in all situations. We are loved and honored. We have been ransom by Ethiopia and Seba. We have been protected by God.

All things work together for our good. There is nothing to fear or be afraid with. We need to trust God and be at peace. He cares and we are dear to Him.

Read;

But Zion said, "The LORD has forsaken me, and my Lord has forgotten me."

"Can a woman forget her nursing child, and not have compassion on the son of her womb? Surely they may forget, yet I will not forget you.

See, I have inscribed you on the palms of My hands; Your walls are continually before Me. Your sons shall make haste; your destroyers and those who laid you waste shall go away from you.

Lift up your eyes, look around and see; all these gather together and come to you. As I live," says the LORD, "You shall surely clothe yourselves with them all as an ornament, and bind them on you as a bride does. (Isaiah 49:14-18)

Do you afraid? Do not let the heart be troubled, believe in God and also in Christ. He is going to prepare a place for us and shall come back and take to Himself. Do not be afraid! He can do everything that is needed for this life and the life to come. Do you believe?

For a good living; salvation and knowledge gain!
B. B. S. LIFE BOOKS.
The Victims of Lifelong Slavery Page

Also by Bernard Benson Sarfo

The Fact Among Facts (1st)
The Fact Among Facts

Standalone
The Youth Murderer
Be Original Not a Copy
The Christians Science or Scholarship
Precious than Paradise
Habit Makes Future
A shelter from storm and rain
The Science of Life
The Strongest Lion Knockback
The Perfect and Inspiring City
Above Hope, Faith and Love
The Hero's Brave Decisions
The Weakest Among Plants
The Hero's Brave Decisions
Doing Above The Ability
The Wisdom Beyond Power And Greatness
Heavier Than the Heavens
The Academics Brains and Recreation Logics
The Strange Voice

The Chaotic World
Don't Miss Your Flight
Let the Nations Ponder
You Are Your Thoughts
I AM has sent me to you
Life Tools
The Fact Among Facts
You Are Glorified
The Victims of Lifelong Slavery

About the Author

Bernard Benson Sarfo is an acquainted architectural designer and a motivational speaker.He is a gifted teacher who continues to motivate and encourage many.

Read more at https://www.amazon.com//author/bbslifebooks.